JANE AUSTEN

Patchwork quilt made by Jane Austen.

JANE AUSTEN

CRESCENT BOOKS
NEW YORK • AVENEL

This edition published 1995 by Crescent Books,
distributed by Random House Value Publishing, Inc.
40 Engelhard Avenue, Avenel, New Jersey 07001.

Random House
New York • Toronto • London • Sydney • Auckland

First published 1993 by Aurum Press Ltd,
25 Bedford Avenue, London WC1B 3AT

Text selection and design copyright © 1993
by Russell Ash & Bernard Higton

A CIP catalog record for this book is available from the Library of Congress.

ISBN 0-517-14255-4

Printed and bound in China by Regent Publishing Services

10 9 8 7 6 5 4 3 2 1

Shakespeare has had neither equal nor second. But among the writers who, in the point which we have noticed, have approached nearest to the manner of the great master, we have no hesitation in placing Jane Austen, a woman of whom England is justly proud. She has given us a multitude of characters, all in a certain sense common-place, all such as we meet every day. Yet they are all as perfectly discriminated from each other as if they were the most eccentric of human beings.

THOMAS BABINGTON MACAULAY

It was the peculiar Misfortune of this Woman to have bad Ministers – since wicked as she herself was, she could not have committed such extensive mischief, had not these vile and abandoned men connived at, and encouraged her in her crimes. I know that it has by many people been asserted and believed that Lord Burleigh, Sir Francis Walsingham, and the rest of those who filled the chief offices of State were deserving, experienced, and able Ministers. But oh! how blinded such Writers and such readers must be to true Merit, to Merit despised, neglected and defamed, if they can persist in such opinions when they reflect that these Men, these boasted Men were such Scandals to their Country and their Sex as to allow and assist their Queen in confining for the space of ninteen years a Woman who if the claims of Relationship and Merit were no avail, yet as a Queen and as one who condescended to place confidence in her, had every reason to expect Assistance and Protection; and at length in allowing Elizabeth to bring this amiable Woman to an untimely, unmerited and scandalous Death. Can any one if he reflects but for a moment on this blot, this everlasting blot upon their Understanding and their Character, allow any praise to Lord Burleigh or Sir Francis Walsingham? Oh! what must this bewitching Princess whose only freind was then the Duke of Norfolk, and whose only ones are now Mr Whitaker, Mrs Lefroy, Mrs Knight and myself, who was abandoned by her son, confined by her Cousin, Abused, reproached and villified by all, what must not her noble mind have suffered when informed that Elizabeth had given orders for her Death! Yet she bore it with a most unshaken fortitude; firm in her Mind; Constant to her Religion; and prepared herself to meet the cruel fate to which she was doomed from conscious Innocence. And yet could you Reader have beleived it possible that some hardened and zealous Protestants have even abused her for that Steadfastness in the Catholic Religion which reflected on her so much credit? But this is a striking proof of their narrow Souls and prejudiced Judgements who accuse her. She was executed in the Great Hall Fortheringay Castle (sacred place!) on Wednesday the 8th of February 1586 – to the everlasting Reproach of Elizabeth, her Ministers, and of England in general.

FROM JANE AUSTEN'S THE HISTORY OF ENGLAND, 1791

ℰARLY ACCLAIM

Also read again, and for the third time at least, Miss Austen's very finely written novel of *Pride and Prejudice*. That young lady had a talent for describing the involvements, and feelings, and characters of ordinary life, which is to me the most wonderful I ever met with. The Big Bow-wow strain I can do myself like any now going; but the exquisite touch, which renders ordinary commonplace things and characters interesting, from the truth of the description and the sentiment, is denied to me. What a pity such a gifted creature died so early!

SIR WALTER SCOTT

The want of elegance is almost the only want in Miss Austen. I have not read her *Mansfield Park*; but it is impossible not to feel in every line of *Pride and Prejudice*, in every word of Elizabeth, the entire want of taste which could produce so pert, so worldly a heroine as the beloved of such a man as Darcy. Wickham is equally bad. Oh! they were just fit for each other, and I cannot forgive that delightful Darcy for parting them. Darcy should have married Jane. He is of all the admirable characters the best designed and the best sustained. I quite agree with you in preferring Miss Austen to Miss Edgeworth. If the former had a little more taste, a little more perception of the graceful, as well as of the humorous, I know not indeed any one to whom I should not prefer her. There is none of the hardness, the cold selfishness, of Miss Edgeworth about her writings; she is in a much better humour with the world; she preaches no sermons; she wants nothing but the *beau-idéal* of the female character to be a perfect novel writer; and perhaps even that *beau-idéal* would only be missed by such a *petite maîtresse* in books as myself, who would

never admit a muse into my library till she had been taught to dance by the Graces.

In Bath, whenever it rained...I thought of Anne Elliott meeting Captain Wentworth...Whenever I got out of breath climbing uphill I thought of that same charming Anne Elliott, and of that ascent from the lower town to the upper, during which all her tribulations cease...I doubt if any one, even Scott himself, has left such perfect impressions of character and place as Jane Austen.

MARY RUSSELL MITFORD TO SIR WILLIAM ELFORD, 20 DECEMBER 1814

I had already made up my mind that *Pride and Prejudice* was the best novel in the English language, – a palm which I only partially withdrew after a second reading of *Ivanhoe*, and did not completely bestow elsewhere till *Esmond* was written.

ANTHONY TROLLOPE

It is a truth universally acknowledged, that a single man in possession of a good fortune must be in want of a wife.

However little known the feelings or views of such a man may be on his first entering a neighbourhood, this truth is so well fixed in the minds of the surrounding families, that he is considered as the rightful property of some one or other of their daughters.

"My dear Mr Bennet," said his lady to him one day, "have you heard that Netherfield Park is let at last?"

Mr Bennet replied that he had not.

"But it is," returned she; "for Mrs Long has just been here, and she told me all about it."

Mr Bennet made no answer.

"Do not you want to know who has taken it?" cried his wife impatiently.

"You want to tell me, and I have no objection to hearing it."

This was invitation enough.

"Why, my dear, you must know, Mrs Long says that Netherfield is taken by a young man of large fortune from the north of England; that he came down on Monday in a chaise and four to see the place, and was so much delighted with it that he agreed with Mr Morris immediately; that he is to take possession before Michaelmas, and some of his servants are to be in the house by the end of next week."

"What is his name?"

"Bingley."

"Is he married or single?"

"Oh! single, my dear, to be sure! A single man of large fortune; four or five thousand a year. What a fine thing for our girls!"

"How so? how can it affect them?"

"My dear Mr Bennet," replied his wife, "how can you be so tiresome! You must know that I am thinking of his marrying one of them."

"Is that his design in settling here?"

"Design! nonsense, how can you talk so! But it is very likely that he may fall in love with one of them, and therefore you must visit him as soon as he comes."

PRIDE AND PREJUDICE

$\mathcal{A}$ Great Park

Elizabeth, as they drove along, watched for the first appearance of Pemberley Woods with some perturbation; and when at length they turned in at the lodge, her spirits were in a high flutter.

The park was very large, and contained great variety of ground. They entered it in one of its lowest points, and drove for some time through a beautiful wood stretching over a wide extent.

Elizabeth's mind was too full for conversation, but she saw and admired every remarkable spot and point of view. They gradually ascended for half a mile, and then found themselves at the top of a considerable eminence, where the wood ceased, and the eye was instantly caught by Pemberley House, situated on the opposite side of a valley, into which the road with some abruptness wound. It was a large, handsome, stone building, standing well on rising ground, and backed by a ridge of high woody hills; – and in front, a stream of some natural importance was swelled into greater, but without any artificial appearance. Its banks were neither formal nor falsely adorned. Elizabeth was delighted. She had never seen a place for which nature had done more, or where natural beauty had been so little counteracted by an awkward taste. They were all of them warm in their admiration; and at that moment she felt that to be mistress of Pemberley might be something!

They descended the hill, crossed the bridge, and drove to the door; and, while examining the nearer aspect of the house, all her apprehension of meeting its owner returned. She dreaded lest the chamber-maid had been mistaken. On applying to see the place, they were admitted into the hall; and Elizabeth, as they waited for the housekeeper, had leisure to wonder at her being where she was.

PRIDE AND PREJUDICE

Mrs Bennet and Kitty walked off, and as soon as they were gone Mr Collins began.

"Believe me, my dear Miss Elizabeth, that your modesty, so far from doing you any disservice, rather adds to your other perfections. You would have been less amiable in my eyes had there not been this little unwillingness; but allow me to assure you that I have your respected Mother's permission for this address. You can hardly doubt the purport of my discourse, however your natural delicacy may lead you to dissemble; my attentions have been too marked to be mistaken. Almost as soon as I entered the house, I singled you out as the companion of my future life. But before I am run away with my feelings on this subject, perhaps it would be advisable for me to state my reasons for marrying – and moreover for coming into Hertfordshire with the design of selecting a wife, as I certainly did."

The idea of Mr Collins, with all his solemn composure, being run away with by his feelings, made Elizabeth so near laughing that she could not use the short pause he allowed in any attempt to stop him farther, and he continued:

"My reasons for marrying are, first, that I think it is a right thing for every clergyman in easy circumstances (like myself) to set the example of matrimony in his parish. Secondly, that I am convinced it will add very greatly to my happiness; and thirdly – which perhaps I ought to have mentioned earlier, that it is the particular advice and recommendation of the very noble lady whom I have the honour of calling patroness. Twice has she condescended to give me her opinion (unasked too!) on this subject; and it was but the very Saturday night before I left Hunsford – between our pools at Quadrille, while Mrs Jenkinson was arranging Miss de Bourgh's footstool, that she said,

'Mr Collins, you must marry. A clergyman like you must marry. Chuse properly, chuse a gentlewoman for my sake.'"…

"To fortune I am perfectly indifferent, and shall make no demand of that nature on your father, since I am well aware that it could not be complied with; and that one thousand pounds in the 4 per cents, which will not be yours till after your mother's decease, is all that you may ever be entitled to. On that head, therefore, I shall be uniformly silent; and you may assure yourself that no ungenerous reproach shall ever pass my lips when we are married."

It was absolutely necessary to interrupt him now.

"You are too hasty, sir," she cried. "You forget that I have made no answer. Let me do it without further loss of time. Accept my thanks for the compliment you are paying me. I am very sensible of the honour of your proposals, but it is impossible for me to do otherwise than decline them."

"I am not now to learn," replied Mr Collins, with a formal wave of the hand, "that it is usual with young ladies to reject the addresses of the man whom they secretly mean to accept, when he first applies for their favour; and that sometimes the refusal is repeated a second or even a third time. I am therefore by no means discouraged by what you have just said, and shall hope to lead you to the altar ere long."

"Upon my word, sir," cried Elizabeth, "your hope is rather an extraordinary one after my declaration. I do assure you that I am not one of those young ladies (if such young ladies there are) who are so daring as to risk their happiness on the chance of being asked a second time. I am perfectly serious in my refusal. You could not make me happy, and I am convinced that I am the last woman in the world who would make you so.

PRIDE AND PREJUDICE

Colonel Fitzwilliam seemed really glad to see them; any thing was a welcome relief to him at Rosings; and Mrs Collins's pretty friend had moreover caught his fancy very much. He now seated himself by her, and talked so agreeably of Kent and Hertfordshire, of travelling and staying at home, of new books and music, that Elizabeth had never been half so well entertained in that room before; and they conversed with so much spirit and flow, as to draw the attention of Lady Catherine herself, as well as of Mr Darcy. His eyes had been soon and repeatedly turned towards them with a look of curiosity; and that her ladyship, after a while, shared the feeling, was more openly acknowledged, for she did not scruple to call out,

"What is that you are saying, Fitzwilliam? What is it you are talking of? What are you telling Miss Bennet? Let me hear what it is."

"We are speaking of music, madam," said he, when no longer able to avoid a reply.

"Of music! Then pray speak aloud. It is of all subjects my delight. I must have my share in the conversation, if you are speaking of music. There are few people in England, I suppose, who have more true enjoyment of music than myself, or a better natural taste. If I had ever learnt, I should have been a great proficient. And so would Anne, if her health had allowed her to apply. I am confident that she would have performed delightfully. How does Georgiana get on, Darcy?"

Mr Darcy spoke with affectionate praise of his sister's proficiency.

"I am very glad to hear such a good account of her," said Lady Catherine; "and pray tell her from me, that she cannot expect to excel, if she does not practise a great deal."

"I assure you, madam," he replied, "that she does not need such advice. She practises very constantly."

"So much the better. It cannot be done too much; and when I next write to her, I shall charge her not to neglect it on any account. I often tell young ladies, that no excellence in music is to be acquired, without constant practice."

ℛ ECOLLECTIONS OF AUNT JANE

As to my aunt's personal appearance, hers was the first face that I can remember thinking pretty... Her face was rather round than long – she had a bright, but not a pink colour – a clear brown complexion and very good hazel eyes... Her hair, a darkish brown, curled naturally – it was in short curls around her face (for *then* ringlets were *not*). She always wore a cap – such was the custom with the ladies who were not quite young – at least of a morning I never saw her without one... I believe my two Aunts were not accounted very good dressers, and were though to have taken to the garb of middle age unnecessarily soon... Her handwriting remains to bear testimony to its own excellence, and every note and letter of hers, was finished off handsomely. There was an art *then* in folding and sealing – no adhesive envelopes made all easy – some people's letters looked always loose and untidy – but *her* paper was sure to take the right folds, and *her* sealing wax to drop in the proper place... Aunt Jane had a regard for her neighbours and felt a kindly interest in their proceedings... They sometimes served for her amusement, but it was her own nonsense that gave zest to the gossip – she never turned *them* into ridicule – she was as far as possible from being censorious or satirical... Her charm to children was great sweetness of manner – she seemed to love you, and you loved her naturally in return.

CAROLINE AUSTEN

Her stature rather exceeded the middle height; her carriage and deportment were quiet but graceful; her features were separately good; their assemblage produced an unrivalled expression of that cheerfulness, sensibility, and benevolence which were her real

Jane Austen painted by her sister Cassandra.

characteristics; her complexion was of the finest texture – it might with truth be said that her eloquent blood spoke through her modest cheek; her voice was sweet; she delivered herself with fluency and precision; indeed, she was formed for elegant and rational society, excelling in conversation as much as in composition.

G. H. LEWES (QUOTING HENRY AUSTEN)

Every morning now brought its regular duties: shops were to be visited; some new part of the town to be looked at; and the Pump-room to be attended, where they paraded up and down for an hour, looking at everybody and speaking to no one. The wish of a numerous acquaintance in Bath was still uppermost with Mrs Allen, and she repeated it after every fresh proof, which every morning brought, of her knowing nobody at all.

They made their appearance in the Lower Rooms; and here fortune was more favourable to our heroine. The master of the ceremonies introduced to her a very gentlemanlike young man as a partner; – his name was Tilney. He seemed to be about four or five and twenty, was rather tall, had a pleasing countenance, a very intelligent and lively eye, and, if not quite handsome, was very near it. His address was good, and Catherine felt herself in high luck. There was little leisure for speaking while they danced; but when they were seated at tea, she found him as agreeable as she had already given him credit for being. He talked with fluency and spirit – and there was an archness and pleasantry in his

manner which interested, though it was hardly understood by her. After chatting some time on such matters as naturally arose from the objects around them, he suddenly addressed her with – "I have hitherto been very remiss, madam, in the proper attentions of a partner here; I have not yet asked you how long you have been in Bath; whether you were ever here before; whether you have been at the Upper Rooms, the theatre, and the concert; and how you like the place altogether. I have been very negligent – but are you now at leisure to satisfy me in these particulars? If you are I will begin directly."

"You need not give yourself that trouble, sir."

"No trouble, I assure you, madam." Then forming his features into a set smile, and affectedly softening his voice, he added, with a simpering air, "Have you been long in Bath, madam?"

"About a week, sir," replied Catherine, trying not to laugh.

NORTHANGER ABBEY

I am sorry to tell you that I am getting very extravagant & spending all my Money; & what is worse for *you*, I have been spending yours too; for in a Linendraper's shop to which I went for check'd muslin, & for which I was obliged to give seven shillings a yard, I was tempted by a pretty coloured muslin, and bought 10 yds of it, on the chance of your liking it; – but at the same time if it should not suit you, you must not think yourself at all obliged to take it; it is only 3/6 per yd, & I should not in the least mind keeping the whole. – In texture, it is just what we prefer, but its resemblance to green cruels I must own is not great, for the pattern is a small red spot...& now I believe I have done all my commissions, except Wedgwood. I liked my walk very much; it was shorter than I had expected, & the weather was delightful. We set off immediately after breakfast & must have reached Grafton House by half past 11, but when we entered the Shop, the whole Counter was thronged, & we waited *full* half an hour before we could be attended to. When we were served, however, I was very well satisfied with my purchases, my Bugle Trimming at 2/4d & 3 pairs of silk stockings for a little less than 12/s a pair. In my way back, who should I meet but Mr Moore, just come from Beckenham. I believe he would have passed me, if I had not made him stop – but we were delighted to meet. I soon found however that he had nothing new to tell me, & then I let him go. Miss Burton has made me a very pretty little Bonnet – & now nothing can satisfy me but I must have a straw hat, of the riding hat shape, like Mrs Tilson's; & a young woman in this Neighbourhood is actually making me one. I am really very shocking; but it will not be dear at a Guinea. Our Pelisses are 17/s each – she charges only 8/s for the making, but the Buttons seem expensive; – *are* expensive, I might have said – for the fact is plain enough. We drank tea again yesterday with the Tilsons, & met the Smiths. – I find all these little parties very pleasant.

LETTER TO CASSANDRA

Thorpe's ideas then all reverted to the merits of his own equipage, and she was called on to admire the spirit and freedom with which his horse moved along, and the ease which his paces, as well as the excellence of the springs, gave the motion of the carriage. She followed him in all his admiration as well as she could. To go before, or beyond him was impossible. His knowledge and her ignorance of the subject, his rapidity of expression, and her diffidence of herself put that out of her power; she could strike out nothing new in commendation, but she readily echoed whatever he chose to assert, and it was finally settled between them without any difficulty, that his equipage was altogether the most complete of its kind in England, his carriage the neatest, his horse the best goer, and himself the best coachman. "You do not really think, Mr Thorpe," said Catherine, venturing after some time to consider the matter as entirely decided, and to offer some little variation on the subject, "that James's gig will break down?"

"Break down! Oh! lord! Did you ever see such a little tittuppy thing in your life? There is not a sound piece of iron about it. The wheels have been fairly worn out these ten years at least – and as for the body! Upon my soul, you might shake it to pieces yourself with a touch. It is the most devilish little rickety business I ever beheld! Thank God! we have got a better. I would not be bound to go two miles in it for fifty thousand pounds."

"Good heavens!" cried Catherine, quite frightened, "then pray let us turn back; they will certainly meet with an accident if we go

on. Do let us turn back, Mr Thorpe; stop and speak to my brother, and tell him how very unsafe it is."

"Unsafe! Oh, lord! what is there in that? they will only get a roll if it does break down; and there is plenty of dirt, it will be excellent falling. Oh, curse it! the carriage is safe enough, if a man knows how to drive it; a thing of that sort in good hands will last above twenty years after it is fairly worn out. Lord bless you! I would undertake for five pounds to drive it to York and back again, without losing a nail."

NORTHANGER ABBEY

CATHERINE AT THE ABBEY

This apartment, to which she had given a date so ancient, a position so awful, proved to be one end of what the General's father had built. There were two other doors in the chamber, leading probably into dressing-closets; but she had no inclination to open either. Would the veil in which Mrs Tilney had last walked, or the volume in which she had last read, remain to tell what nothing else was allowed to whisper? No: whatever might have been the General's crimes, he had certainly too much wit to let them sue for detection. She was sick of exploring, and desired but to be safe in her own room, with her own heart only privy to its folly; and she was on the point of retreating as softly as she had entered, when the sound of footsteps, she could hardly tell where, made her pause and tremble. To be found there, even by a servant, would be unpleasant; but by the General (and he seemed always at hand when least wanted), much worse! She listened – the sound had ceased; and resolving not to lose a moment, she passed through and closed the door. At that instant a door underneath was hastily opened; someone seemed with swift steps to ascend the stairs, by the head of which she had yet to pass before she could gain the gallery. She had no power to move. With a feeling of terror not very definable, she fixed her eyes on the staircase, and in a few moments it gave Henry to her view. "Mr Tilney!" she exclaimed in a voice of more than common astonishment. He looked astonished too. "Good God!" she continued, not attending to his address, "how came you here? – how came you up that staircase?"

"How came I up that staircase!" he replied, greatly surprised. "Because it is my nearest way from the stable-yard to my own chamber: and why should I not come up it?"

If a rainy morning deprived them of other enjoyments, they were still resolute in meeting in defiance of wet and dirt, and shut themselves up, to read novels together. Yes, novels; – for I will not adopt that ungenerous and impolitic custom so common with novel-writers, of degrading by their contemptuous censure the very performances, to the number of which they are themselves adding – joining with their greatest enemies in bestowing the harshest epithets on such works, and scarcely ever permitting them to be read by their own heroine, who, if she accidentally take up a novel, is sure to turn over its insipid pages with disgust. Alas! if the heroine of one novel be not patronized by the heroine of another, from whom can she expect protection and regard? I cannot approve of it. Let us leave it to the Reviewers to abuse such effusions of fancy at their leisure, and over every new novel to talk in threadbare strains of the trash with which the press now groans. Let us not desert one another; we are an injured body. Although our productions have afforded more extensive and unaffected pleasure than those of any other literary corporation in the world, no species of composition had been so much decried. From pride, ignorance, or fashion, our foes are almost as many as our readers. And while the abilities of the nine-hundredth abridger of the *History of England*, or of the man who collects and publishes in a volume some dozen lines of Milton, Pope, and Prior, with a paper from the *Spectator*, and a chapter from Sterne, are eulogized by a thousand pens, – there seems almost a general wish of decrying the capacity and under-valuing the labour of the novelist, and of slighting the performances which have only genius, wit, and taste to recommend

them. "I am no novel-reader – I seldom look into novels – Do not imagine that *I* often read novels – It is really very well for a novel." – Such is the common cant. – "And what are you reading, Miss ——-?" "Oh! it is only a novel!" replies the young lady; while she lays down her book with affected indifference, or momentary shame. – "It is only Cecilia, or Camilla, or Belinda;" or, in short, only some work in which the greatest powers of the mind are displayed, in which the most thorough knowledge of human nature, the happiest delineation of its varieties, the liveliest effusions of wit and humour, are conveyed to the world in the best-chosen language.

NORTHANGER ABBEY

First and foremost let Jane Austen be named, the greatest artist that has ever written, using the term to signify the most perfect mastery over the means to her end. There are heights and depths in human nature Miss Austen has never scaled nor fathomed, there are worlds of passionate existence into which she has never set foot; but although this is obvious to every reader, it is equally obvious that she has risked no failures by attempting to delineate that which she had not seen. Her circle may be restricted, but it is complete. Her world is a perfect orb, and vital. Life, as it presents itself to an English gentlewoman peacefully yet actively engaged in her quiet village, is mirrored in her works with a purity and fidelity that must endow them with interest for all time. To read one of her books is like an actual experience of life: you know the people as if you had lived with them, and you feel something of personal affection towards them. The marvellous reality and subtle distinctive traits noticeable in her portraits has led Macaulay to call her a prose Shakespeare. If the whole force of the distinction which lies in that epithet *prose* be fairly appreciated, no one, we think, will dispute the compliment; for out of Shakespeare it would be difficult to find characters so typical yet so nicely demarcated within the limits of their kind. We do not find such profound psychological insight as may be found in George Sand (not to mention male writers), but taking the type to which the characters belong, we see the most intimate and accurate knowledge in all Miss Austen's creations.

GEORGE ELIOT, WESTMINSTER REVIEW, JULY 1852

Then whiled away the evening over one of Miss Austen's novels; there is a truth of painting in her writings which always delights me. They do not it is true get above the middle classes of society. But there she is inimitable.

SIR WALTER SCOTT

Miss Austen has generally but an indifferent story to tell, but her art of telling it is incomparable. Her characters, never ideal, are not of an eminently attractive order; but her dramatic ventri-loquism and power of presentation is little less than marvellous. Macaulay declares his opinion that in this respect she is second only to Shakespeare.

G. H. LEWES

She is a miniaturist, but never two-dimensional. All her charac-ters are round, or capable of rotundity...All the Jane Austen characters are ready for an extended life, for a life which the scheme of her books seldom requires them to lead, and that is why they lead their actual lives so satisfactorily.

E. M. FORSTER

$\mathcal{A}$ Gentleman Appears

They gaily ascended the downs, rejoicing in their own penetration at every glimpse of blue sky; and when they caught in their faces the animating gales of an high south-westerly wind, they pitied the fears which had prevented their mother and Elinor from sharing such delightful sensations.

"Is there a felicity in the world," said Marianne, "superior to this? – Margaret, we will walk here at least two hours."

Margaret agreed, and they pursued their way against the wind, resisting it with laughing delight for about twenty minutes longer, when suddenly the clouds united over their heads, and a driving rain set full in their face. – Chagrined and surprised, they were obliged, though unwillingly, to turn back, for no shelter was nearer than their own house. One consolation however remained for them, to which the exigence of the moment gave more than usual propriety; it was that of running with all possible speed down the steep side of the hill which led immediately to their garden gate.

They set off. Marianne had at first the advantage, but a false step brought her suddenly to the ground, and Margaret, unable to stop herself to assist her, was involuntarily hurried along, and reached the bottom in safety.

A gentleman carrying a gun, with two pointers playing round him, was passing up the hill and within a few yards of Marianne, when her accident happened. He put down his gun and ran to her assistance. She had raised herself from the ground, but her foot had been twisted in the fall, and she was scarcely able to stand. The gentleman offered his services, and perceiving that her modesty declined what her situation rendered necessary, took her up in his arms without farther delay, and carried her down

the hill. Then passing through the garden, the gate of which had been left open by Margaret, he bore her directly into the house, whither Margaret was just arrived, and quitted not his hold till he had seated her in a chair in the parlour.

SENSE AND SENSIBILITY

Have you read *Sense and Sensibility*? It is a clever novel. They were full of it at Althorp, and though it ends stupidly, I was much amused by it.

LADY BESSBOROUGH, LETTER TO LORD GOWER, 25 NOVEMBER 1811

Elinor's Company

B ut Elinor – How are *her* feelings to be described? – From the moment of learning that Lucy was married to another, that Edward was free, to the moment of his justifying the hopes which had so instantly followed, she was everything by turns but tranquil. But when the second moment had passed, when she found every doubt, every solicitude removed, compared her situation with what so lately it had been, – saw him honourably released from his former engagement, saw him instantly profiting by the release, to address herself and declare an affection as tender, as constant as she had ever supposed it to be, – she was oppressed, she was overcome by her own felicity; – and happily disposed as is the human mind to be easily familiarized with any change for the better, it required several hours to give sedateness to her spirits, or any degree of tranquillity to her heart.

Edward was now fixed at the cottage at least for a week; – for whatever other claims might be made on him, it was impossible that less than a week should be given up to enjoyment of Elinor's company, or suffice to say half that was to be said of the past, the present, and the future; – for though a very few hours spent in the hard labour of incessant talking will dispatch more subjects than can really be in common between any two rational creatures, yet with lovers it is different. Between *them* no subject is finished, no communication is even made, till it has been made at least twenty times over.

SENSE AND SENSIBILITY

A VISIT FROM JANE AUSTEN

Jane Austen's needle case.

I remember that when Aunt Jane came to us at Godmersham she used to bring the manuscript of whatever novel she was writing with her, and would shut herself up with my elder sisters in one of the bedrooms to read them aloud. I and the younger ones used to hear peals of laughter through the door, and thought it very hard that we should be shut out from what was so delightful... I also remember [she added] how Aunt Jane would sit quietly working [which meant sewing] beside the fire in the library, saying nothing for a good while, and then would suddenly burst out laughing, jump up and run across the room to a table where pens and paper were lying, write something down, and then come back across to the fire and go on quietly working as before.

MARIANNE KNIGHT

Cork Street: Tuesday morn [August 1796]

My dear Cassandra

Here I am once more in this scene of dissipation and vice, and I begin already to find my morals corrupted. We reached Staines yesterday, I do not (know) when, without suffering so much from the heat as I had hoped to do. We set off again this morning at seven o'clock, and had a very pleasant drive, as the morning was cloudy and perfectly cool. I came all the way in the chaise from Hertford Bridge.

Edward and Frank are both gone out to seek their fortunes; the latter is to return soon and help us seek ours. The former we shall never see again. We are to be at Astley's to-night, which I am glad of. Edward has heard from Henry this morning. He has not been at the races at all, unless his driving Miss Pearson over to Rowling one day can be so called. We shall find him there on Thursday.

I hope you are all alive after our melancholy parting yesterday, and that you pursued your intended avocation with success. God bless you! I must leave off, for we are going out.

Yours very affectionately,

J. Austen

LETTER TO CASSANDRA

A GENTLEMAN'S SEAT

Tom Bertram must have been thought pleasant, indeed, at any rate; he was the sort of young man to be generally liked, his agreeableness was of the kind to be oftener found agreeable than some endowments of a higher stamp, for he had easy manners, excellent spirits, a large acquaintance, and a great deal to say; and the reversion of Mansfield Park, and a baronetcy, did no harm to all this. Miss Crawford soon felt that he and his situation might do. She looked about her with due consideration, and found almost everything in his favour: a park, a real park, five miles round, a spacious modern-built house, so well placed and well screened as to deserve to be in any collection of engravings of gentlemen's seats in the kingdom, and wanting only to be completely new furnished – pleasant sisters, a quiet mother, and an agreeable man himself – with the advantage of being tied up from much gaming at present by a promise to his father, and of being Sir Thomas hereafter. It might do very well; she believed she should accept him; and she began accordingly to interest herself a little about the horse which he had to run at the B—— races.

These races were to call him away not long after their acquaintance began; and as it appeared that the family did not, from his usual goings on, expect him back again for many weeks, it would bring his passion to an early proof.

MANSFIELD PARK

$\mathcal{F}$ANNY PRICE

"No, my plan is to make Fanny Price in love with me."

"Fanny Price! Nonsense! No, no. You ought to be satisfied with her two cousins."

"But I cannot be satisfied without Fanny Price, without making a small hole in Fanny Price's heart. You do not seem properly aware of her claims to notice. When we talked of her last night, you none of you seemed sensible of the wonderful improvement that has taken place in her looks within the last six weeks. You see her every day, and therefore do not notice it; but I assure you she is quite a different creature from what she was in the autumn. She was then merely a quiet, modest, not plain-looking girl, but she is now absolutely pretty. I used to think she had neither complexion nor countenance; but in that soft skin of hers, so frequently tinged with a blush as it was yesterday, there is decided beauty; and from what I observed of her eyes and mouth, I do not despair of their being capable of expression enough when she has anything to express. And then, her air, her manner, her *tout ensemble*, is so indescribably improved! She must be grown two inches, at least, since October."

MANSFIELD PARK

*T*HE NOTE
....

"I am very much obliged to you, my dear Miss Crawford, for your kind congratulations, as far as they relate to my dearest William. The rest of your note I know means nothing; but I am so unequal to anything of the sort, that I hope you will excuse my begging you to take no farther notice. I have seen too much of Mr Crawford not to understand his manners; if he understood me as well, he would, I dare say, behave differently. I do not know what I write, but it would be a great favour of you never to mention the subject again. With thanks for the honour of your note, I remain, dear Miss Crawford, etc., etc."

The conclusion was scarcely intelligible from increasing fright, for she found that Mr Crawford, under pretence of receiving the note, was coming towards her.

"You cannot think I mean to hurry you," said he, in an undervoice, perceiving the amazing trepidation with which she made up the note; "you cannot think I have any such object. Do not hurry yourself, I entreat."

"Oh! I thank you; I have quite done, just done; it will be ready in a moment; I am very much obliged to you; if you will be so good as to give *that* to Miss Crawford."

The note was held out, and must be taken; and as she instantly and with averted eyes walked towards the fireplace, where sat the others, he had nothing to do but go in good earnest.

Fanny thought she had never known a day of greater agitation, both of pain and pleasure; but happily the pleasure was not of a sort to die with the day; for every day would restore the knowledge of William's advancement, whereas the pain, she hoped, would return no more. She had no doubt that her note must appear excessively ill-written, that the language would disgrace a

child, for her distress had allowed no arrangement; but at least it would assure them both of her being neither imposed on nor gratified by Mr Crawford's attentions.

MANSFIELD PARK

The day was uncommonly lovely. It was really March; but it was April in its mild air, brisk soft wind, and bright sun, occasionally clouded for a minute; and everything looked so beautiful under the influence of such a sky, the effects of the shadows pursuing each other on the ships at Spithead and the island beyond, with the ever-varying hues of the sea, now at high water, dancing in its glee and dashing against the ramparts with so fine a sound, produced altogether such a combination of charms for Fanny, as made her gradually almost careless of the circumstances under which she felt them. Nay, had she been without his arm, she would soon have known that she needed it, for she wanted strength for a two hours' saunter of this kind, coming, as it generally did, upon a week's previous inactivity. Fanny was beginning to feel the effect of being debarred from her usual exercise; she had lost ground as to health since her being in Portsmouth; and but for Mr Crawford and the beauty of the weather would soon have been knocked up now.

The loveliness of the day, and of the view, he felt like herself. They often stopt with the same sentiment and taste, leaning against the wall, some minutes, to look and admire; and considering he was not Edmund, Fanny could not but allow that he was sufficiently open to the charms of nature, and very well able to express his admiration. She had a few tender reveries now and then, which he could sometimes take advantage of to look in her face without detection; and the result of these looks was, that though as bewitching as ever, her face was less blooming than it ought to be. She said she was very well, and did not like to be supposed otherwise; but take it all in all, he was convinced that her present residence could not be comfortable, and therefore could not be salutary for her, and he was growing anxious for her being again at Mansfield, where her own happiness, and his in seeing her, must be so much greater.

~~~~

It was sad to Fanny to lose all the pleasures of spring. She had not known before what pleasures she had to lose in passing March and April in a town. She had not known before how much the beginnings and progress of vegetation had delighted her. What animation, both of body and mind, she had derived from watching the advance of that season which cannot, in spite of its capriciousness, be unlovely, and seeing its increasing beauties from the earliest flowers in the warmest divisions of her aunt's garden, to the opening of leaves of her uncle's plantations, and the glory of his woods. To be losing such pleasures was no trifle; to be losing them because she was in the midst of closeness and noise, to have confinement, bad air, bad smells, substituted for liberty, freshness, fragrance and verdure, was infinitely worse: but even these incitements to regret were feeble, compared with what arose from the conviction of being missed by her best friends, and the longing to be useful to those who were wanting her!

Could she have been at home, she might have been of service to every creature in the house. She felt that she must have been of use to all. To all she must have saved some trouble of head or hand; and were it only in supporting the spirits of her aunt Bertram, keeping her from the evil of solitude, or the still greater evil of a restless, officious companion, too apt to be heightening danger in order to heighten her own importance, her being there would have been a general good.

MANSFIELD PARK

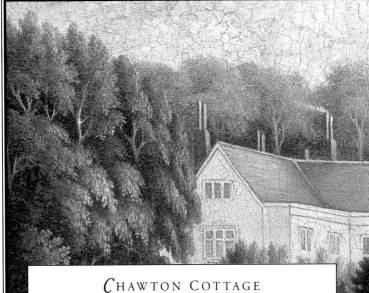

CHAWTON COTTAGE

A good-sized entrance and two sitting-rooms made the length of the house, intended originally to look upon the road, but the large drawing-room window was blocked up and turned into a book-case, and another opened at the side which gave to view only turf and trees, as a high wooden fence and hornbeam hedge shut out the Winchester road, which skirted the whole length of the little domain. Trees were planted each side to form a shrubbery walk, carried round the enclosure, which gave a sufficient space for ladies' exercise. There was a pleasant irregular mixture of hedgerow, and gravel walk, and orchard, and long grass for mowing.

EDWARD AUSTEN-LEIGH

Chawton House: the cottage is in the village near by.

H e moved a few steps nearer, and those few steps were enough to prove in how gentlemanlike a manner, with what natural grace, he must have danced, would he but take the trouble. Whenever she caught his eye, she forced him to smile; but in general he was looking grave. She wished he could love a ball-room better, and could like Frank Churchill better. He seemed often observing her. She must not flatter herself that he thought of her dancing; but if he were criticising her behaviour, she did not feel afraid. There was nothing like flirtation between her and her partner. They seemed more like cheerful easy friends than lovers. That Frank Churchill thought less of her than he had done was indubitable.

The ball proceeded pleasantly. The anxious cares, the incessant attentions of Mrs Weston were not thrown away. Everybody seemed happy; and the praise of being a delightful ball, which is seldom bestowed till after a ball has ceased to be, was repeatedly given in the very beginning of the existence of this. Of very important, very recordable events, it was not more productive than such meetings usually are. There was one, however, which Emma thought something of. – The two last dances before supper were begun, and Harriet had no partner; – the only young lady sitting down; and so equal had been hitherto the number of dancers, that how there could be any one disengaged was the wonder. But Emma's wonder lessened soon afterwards, on seeing Mr Elton sauntering about. He would not ask Harriet to dance, if it were possible to be avoided; she was sure he would not – and she was expecting him every moment to escape into the card-room.

Escape, however, was not his plan. He came to the part of the

room where the sitters-by were collected, spoke to some, and walked about in front of them, as if to show his liberty, and his resolution of maintaining it.

EMMA

I have been reading *Emma*, which is excellent; there is no story whatever and the heroine is no better than other people; but the characters are so true to life, and her style is so piquant, that it does not need the adventitious aids of mystery and adventure.

SUSAN FERRIER, LETTER TO MISS CLAVERING, 1816

Whoever is fond of an amusing, inoffensive, and well-principled novel, will be well pleased with the perusal of *Emma*. It rarely happens that in a production of this nature we have so little to find fault with.

THE BRITISH CRITIC, JULY 1816

*E*MMA AT DONWELL ABBEY

It was hot; and after walking some time over the gardens in a scattered, dispersed way, scarcely any three together, they insensibly followed one another to the delicious shade of a broad short avenue of limes, which, stretching beyond the garden at an equal distance from the river, seemed the finish of the pleasure grounds. It led to nothing; nothing but a view at the end over a low stone wall with high pillars, which seemed intended, in their erection, to give the appearance of an approach to the house, which never had been there. Disputable, however, as might be the taste of such a termination, it was in itself a charming walk and the view which closed it extremely pretty. The considerable slope, at nearly the foot of which the Abbey stood, gradually acquired a steeper form beyond its grounds; and at half a mile distant was a bank of considerable abruptness and grandeur, well clothed with wood, and at the bottom of this bank, favourably placed and sheltered, rose the Abbey Mill Farm, with meadows in front, and the river making a close and handsome curve around it.

It was a sweet view – sweet to the eye and the mind. English verdure, English culture, English comfort, seen under a sun bright, without being oppressive.

EMMA

Mr Knightley Proposes

....

"You are going in, I suppose?" said he.

"No," replied Emma, quite confirmed by the depressed manner in which he still spoke, "I should like to take another turn. Mr Perry is not gone." And, after proceeding a few steps, she added – "I stopped you ungraciously, just now, Mr Knightley, and, I am afraid, gave you pain. But if you have any wish to speak openly to me as a friend, or to ask my opinion of anything that you may have in contemplation – as a friend, indeed, you may command me. I will hear whatever you like. I will tell you exactly what I think."

"As a friend!" repeated Mr Knightley. "Emma, that, I fear, is a word – no, I have no wish. Stay, yes, why should I hesitate? I have gone too far already for concealment. Emma, I accept your offer, extraordinary as it may seem, I accept it, and refer myself to you as a friend. Tell me, then, have I no chance of ever succeeding?"

He stopped in his earnestness to look the question, and the expression of his eyes overpowered her.

"My dearest Emma," said he, "for dearest you will always be, whatever the event of this hour's conversation, my dearest, most beloved Emma – tell me at once. Say "No," if it is to be said." She could really say nothing. "You are silent," he cried, with great animation; "absolutely silent! at present I ask no more."

Emma was almost ready to sink under the agitation of this moment. The dread of being awakened from the happiest dream was perhaps the most prominent feeling.

Emma

C.E. Brock. 1898.

'*I* DANCED THEM ALL'

O ur ball was very thin, but by no means unpleasant. There
were thirty-one people, and only eleven ladies out of the
number, and but five single women in the room. Of the gentlemen present you may have some idea from the list of my partners
– Mr Wood, G. Lefroy, Rice, a Mr Butcher (belonging to the
Temples, a sailor and not of the 11th Light Dragoons), Mr Tem-
ple (not the horrid one), Mr Wm. Orde (cousin to the Kingsclere
man), Mr John Harwood, and Mr Calland, who appeared as
usual with his hat in his hand, and stood every now and then
behind Catherine and me to be talked to and abused for not

dancing. We teased him, however, into it at last. I was very glad to see him again after so long a separation, and he was altogether rather the genius and flirt of the evening. He enquired after you.

There were twenty dances, and I danced them all, and without any fatigue. I was glad to find myself capable of dancing so much, and with so much satisfaction as I did; from my slender enjoyment of the Ashford balls (as assemblies for dancing) I had not thought myself equal to it, but in cold weather and with few couples I fancy I could just as well dance for a week together as for half an hour. My black cap was openly admired by Mrs Lefroy, and secretly I imagine by everybody else in the room.

JANE AUSTEN, LETTER TO CASSANDRA

LYME REGIS

It was so much past noon before the two carriages, Mr Musgrove's coach containing the four ladies, and Charles's curricle, in which he drove Captain Wentworth, were descending the long hill into Lyme, and entering upon the still steeper street of the town itself, that it was very evident they would not have more than time for looking about them, before the light and warmth of the day were gone.

After securing accommodations, and ordering a dinner at one of the inns, the next thing to be done was unquestionably to walk directly down to the sea. They were come too late in the year for any amusement or variety which Lyme, as a public place, might offer. The rooms were shut up, the lodgers almost all gone, scarcely any family but of the residents left; and, as there is nothing to admire in the buildings themselves, the remarkable situation of the town, the principal street almost hurrying into the water, the walk to the Cobb, skirting round the pleasant little bay, which, in the season, is animated with bathing machines and company; the Cobb itself, its old wonders and new improvements, with the very beautiful line of cliffs stretching out to the east of the town, are what the stranger's eye will seek; and a very strange stranger it must be, who does not see charms in the immediate environs of Lyme, to make him wish to know it better. The scenes in its neighbourhood, Charmouth, with its high grounds and extensive sweeps of country, and still more, its sweet, retired bay, backed by dark cliffs, where fragments of low rock among the sands, make it the happiest spot for watching the flow of the tide, for sitting in unwearied contemplation; the wooded varieties of the cheerful village of Up Lyme; and, above

all, Pinny, with its green chasms between romantic rocks, where the scattered forest trees and orchards of luxuriant growth, declare that many a generation must have passed away since the first partial falling of the cliff prepared the ground for such a state, where a scene so wonderful and so lovely is exhibited, as may more than equal any of the resembling scenes of the far-famed Isle of Wight.

PERSUASION

On August 23rd [1867] my father left [Haslemere] for Bridport. He was led on to Lyme by the description of the place in Miss Austen's *Persuasion*, walking thither the nine miles over the hills from Bridport. On his arrival he called on Palgrave, and refusing all refreshment, he said at once: "Now take me to the Cobb, and show me the steps from which Louisa Musgrove fell". Palgrave and he then walked to the undercliff.

LORD TENNYSON, A MEMOIR BY HIS SON

There was too much wind to make the high part of the new Cobb pleasant for the ladies, and they agreed to get down the steps to the lower, and all were contented to pass quietly and carefully down the steep flight, excepting Louisa; she must be jumped down them by Captain Wentworth. In all their walks he had had to jump her from the stiles; the sensation was delightful to her. The hardness of the pavement for her feet made him less willing upon the present occasion; he did it, however. She was safely down, and instantly to show her enjoyment, ran up the steps to be jumped down again. He advised her against it, thought the jar too great; but no, he reasoned and talked in vain, she smiled and said, "I am determined I will:" he put out his hands; she was too precipitate by half a second, she fell on the pavement on the Lower Cobb, and was taken up lifeless! There was no wound, no blood, no visible bruise; but her eyes were closed, she breathed not, her face was like death. The horror of that moment to all who stood around!

Captain Wentworth, who had caught her up, knelt with her in his arms, looking on her with a face as pallid as her own in an agony of silence. "She is dead! she is dead!" screamed Mary, catching hold of her husband, and contributing with his own horror to make him immoveable; and in another moment, Henrietta, sinking under the conviction, lost her senses too, and would have fallen on the steps but for Captain Benwick and Anne, who caught and supported her between them.

"Is there no one to help me?" were the first words which burst from Captain Wentworth, in a tone of despair, and as if all his own strength were gone.

"Go to him, go to him," cried Anne, "for heaven's sake go to

him. I can support her myself. Leave me, and go to him. Rub her
hands, rub her temples; here are salts: take them, take them."

Captain Benwick obeyed, and Charles at the same moment dis-
engaging himself from his wife, they were both with him; and
Louisa was raised up and supported more firmly between them,
and everything was done that Anne had prompted, but in vain;
while Captain Wentworth, staggering against the wall for his support, exclaimed in the bitterest agony –

"Oh God! her father and mother!"

"A surgeon!" said Anne.

The Elliotts in Bath

Sir Walter had taken a very good house in Camden Place, a lofty dignified situation, such as becomes a man of consequence; and both he and Elizabeth were settled there, much to their satisfaction.

Anne entered it with a sinking heart, anticipating an imprisonment of many months, and anxiously saying to herself, "Oh! when shall I leave you again?" A degree of unexpected cordiality, however, in the welcome she received, did her good. Her father and sister were glad to see her, for the sake of shewing her the house and furniture, and met her with kindness. Her making a fourth, when they sat down to dinner, was noticed as an advantage....

They had the pleasure of assuring her that Bath more than answered their expectations in every respect. Their house was undoubtedly the best in Camden Place, their drawing-rooms had many decided advantages over all the others which they had either seen or heard of, and the superiority was not less in the style of the fitting-up or the taste of the furniture. Their acquaintance was exceedingly sought after. Everybody was wanting to visit them. They had drawn back from many introductions, and still were perpetually having cards left by people of whom they knew nothing.

Here were funds of enjoyment! Could Anne wonder that her father and sister were happy? She might not wonder, but she must sigh that her father should feel no degradation in his change, should see nothing to regret in the duties and dignity of the resident landholder, should find so much to be vain of in the littlenesses of a town; and she must sigh, and smile, and wonder too, as Elizabeth threw open the folding-doors, and walked with exultation from one drawing-room to the other, boasting of their space: at the possibility of that woman, who had been mistress of Kellynch Hall, finding extent to be proud of between two walls, perhaps thirty feet asunder.

But this was not all which they had to make them happy. They had Mr Elliot too.

PERSUASION

*I*N PRAISE OF JANE AUSTEN

The author's knowledge of the world, and the peculiar tact with which she presents characters that the reader cannot fail to recognize, reminds us something of the merits of the Flemish school of painting. The subjects are not often elegant, and certainly never grand; but they are finished up to nature, and with a precision which delights the reader.

SIR WALTER SCOTT

Nothing but a mind of this subtle, delicate, speculative temper, could have set before us pictures which are at once so refined and so trenchant, so softly feminine and polite, and so remorselessly true.

MRS OLIPHANT

Surely no man has surpassed Miss Austen as a delineator of common life? Her range, to be sure, is limited; but her art is perfect.

She does not touch those profounder and more impassioned chords which vibrate to the heart's core – never ascends to its grand or heroic movements, nor descends to its deeper throes and agonies; but in all she attempts she is uniformly and completely successful.

It is curious too, and worthy of a passing remark, that women have achieved success in every department of fiction but that of humour. They deal, no doubt, in sly humorous touches often enough; but the broad provinces of that great domain are almost uninvaded by them; beyond the outskirts, and open borders, they have never ventured to pass. Compare Miss Austen, Miss Ferrier, and Miss Edgeworth, with the lusty mirth and riotous humour of Shakespeare, Rabelais, Butler, Swift, Fielding, Smollett, or Dickens and Thackeray. It is like comparing a quiet smile with the inextinguishable 'laughter' of the Homeric gods!

GEORGE HENRY LEWES, EDINBURGH REVIEW, JANUARY 1850

I am amusing myself with Miss Austen's novels. She has great power and discrimination in delineating common-place people; and her writings are a capital picture of real life, with all the little wheels and machinery laid bare like a patent clock.

HENRY WADSWORTH LONGFELLOW

She is my favourite author! I read and re-read, the mouth open and the mind closed. Shut up in measureless content, I greet her by the name of most kind hostess, while criticism slumbers.

E. M. FORSTER

63

$\mathcal{P}$ICTURE ACKNOWLEDGEMENTS

Abbot Hall Art Gallery, Kendal (A.S. Clay Collection): 9, 29.
Jane Austen's House, Chawton: 2, 36 (top), 46–47.
Bridgeman Art Library: 5, 6, 10 (Victoria & Albert Museum),
21 (Victoria Art Gallery, Bath), 25 (Iona Antiques, London),
30 and back jacket, 36 (King Street Galleries, London), 49 &
50–51 (John Noot Galleries, Broadway), 54–55 (City of Bristol
Museum & Art Gallery), 41 (Agnew & Sons).
British Library: 37.
Mary Evans Picture Library: 31, 38–39, 43.
Fine Art Photographic Library: back jacket (top).
Robert Harding Picture Library/The Great-Grandsons of
Admiral Sir Francis Austen: 19 and back jacket.
Mansell Collection: 20 and front jacket (top left), 22, 57, 60.
Wallace Collection: 11.
The Dean and Chapter, Winchester Cathedral: 3.
Private collection: all others.